LOVE
LIFE
&
LIVING

Frank Seiden

ISBN 978-1-959457-23-7

Published by Blue Jay Ink
Ojai, California
bluejayink.com

LOVE

Our 50th Anniversary

Earth has roamed for fifty rounds
Stars sparkled blessings down
Moon shone its soulful nights
Since you donned your wedding crown

Milky Way wove a bridal veil
Saturn spun a sensuous ring
Wind crooned a marriage march
Heaven's host did strongly sing

We flew among comets
Winged on celestial song
Two young bodies joined us
Their orbits smooth and strong

We circled in the firmament
Left the glisten of our trail
It is a memory for young ones
Our life, our love, our tale.

July 31, 2006
Rev. 8/9/06, 9/13/06

A Life Loved

A song sung in morning
flows 'til evening refrain
A song sung in sunshine
changes color in rain

A seed sown in sunshine
bursts open in rain
A seed sown in morning
warms 'til evening refrain

A caress in morning
grows 'til evening refrain
A caress in sunshine
shelters from rain

A Poet's Tale

Ah, the wonderful things I write!
I give them to share.
Meter like Mozart; rhymes with a bite;
brilliantly aware.

I wrote of love, my ardor sweet.
Her hand is what I sought.
She read wide eyed, rose to her feet —
her slap is what I caught.

I wrote a ballad of my tale
of unrequited love,
of pangs of pain that I should fail
to be what she dreamed of.

My ballad cried my heart's despair.
Tears came to my eye.
I used a metaphor to bare
The anguish in my cry.

I brought it to a publisher,
a gal without romance.
She laughed aloud. With caustic slur
said why I had no chance.

I sold it to a hard rock group, its
beauty they'd enhance.
When they sang, that howling troupe,
kids would laugh and dance.

She heard their song, my lady fair,
and said it wasn't true;
unless I gave her half my share,
she had grounds to sue.

I've learned a lesson from all this
that, when you write too well,
a jealous world will go amiss
and pack you off to hell.

Their Music
(Bob & Zena)

A cello sings a concerto of life —
heart strings resonate
to a bow drawn by caressing fingers.
The song is harmonized
by a photographer
who sees the world as it is,
yet mounts his camera on angel's wings,
focuses on the world as it should be
and shows us heavenly hues
that picture their music.

Celebration

I celebrate life when
I help a baby walk,
make it laugh while changing a messy diaper;
think a gaggle of newly hatched goslings is cute
while they waddle in line between the goose and gander
without thinking about the droppings
I'll be stepping on tomorrow;
listen to my daughter laugh,
watch her dance a waltz;
watch my son and daughter-in-law cook dinner,
play with our grandsons;
hold my wife's hand
as we walk on the beach.

March 20, 1998
Rev, March 27, 1998

Len & Ethel
For Your 60th Anniversary

Sixty years of springtime
flowers never fade.
Rainbows follow any storm
every hue and shade.

There is no sunset in your day
only sunrise in reverse.
Star rise beams uplifting dreams;
your dreams are life in verse.

Your smiles warm us.
Your laughter joys our ears.
We thank you living lessons
for the blessing of your years.

For Valentine's Day

There's a day to show our love,
a day when hearts entwine.
A day I pledge that I am yours
and you pledge you are mine.
Let that day be every day,
not just once a year.
Hear it when I say your name,
a sound our love makes dear.

February 13, 2019

The Lost Speech

Vainly he searched his brain for the speech
he had practiced and perfected for over a week.
Laboriously he pulled his velcro tongue
loose from his dry cotton palate.

He told his body to stop sweating,
wouldn't let her hand
touch his clammy palm.
He clenched his knuckles white.

His melodic baritone voice
cracked and squeaked
as he floundered out
some fatuous phrases.

She listened quietly,
her dark brown eyes attentive.
His churning stomach said,
"How could she possibly say 'Yes'
to such a pathetic proposal?"

May 5, 1998 Rev. 5/12/98

A Grain of Time Suspended

Earth
Sleepy sun snuggles into bed.
Misty breath of her drowsy yawn
closes the rose, lifts robin's wings to nest,
draws the deer to evening drink,
lulls the wind to rest,
wakes the frog to chorus,
the firefly to fairy games,
the horned owl to hunt.

Heavens
The glow from sun's drowsy eye
colors cumulus clouds pink and purple
against a blue white sky.
Her eye quickly closes;
her last limb is tucked from sight.
Twinkling dots draw imaginary pictures.
Night's lantern bathes Earth in silvery white light.

Lovers
Sitting, side pressed to side
arms around waists
heads tilted to touching,
man and woman enfold the song of solitude,
embrace the intimacy of darkness.
Moonglow eyes sparkle replies to fireflies.

August 5, 2000
Rev. 11/7/00, 11/?/00, 8/18/02; 4/24/06

Harmony

Souls sing dual flute harmony
as summer wings soaring
on life lifting currents
from flutes in sympathetic resonance.
Notes play with chords
strum a guitar strung with laughter.

Two streams play into one
through roiling rapids and profound pools
shine the sun's prism
sing of peace to the mystic moon
and sleepy stars.

Two woodland spirits
pipe a prayer of love
to deer, bear, beaver.
The nightingale listens
as two hearts harmonize
in moon mood rhythm
dreams and truth entwined.

February 10, 2000, Rev. 3/15/00

Into Togetherness

Two paths meet in
    time
    space
    pulse
    passion
Paths set by
    plan
    perseverence
    fortune

Two streams sprout from mountain springs
    gravitate to fate
They touch
    feel each other's energy
    taste each other's sweetness
    see each other's soul
Quickly waters
    move together
    play together
    become one

Flow through rocky rapids, peaceful pools
Give life to
    flora
    fauna
    mother earth
Give life to new life

May your flow to the sea of infinity
pass through
    lush forest
    bee buzzing meadow
in the light of
    a smiling sun
    sparkling stars
in the light of the Giver of Light

You are like young eagles in
    majesty
    dignity
    power
Your eyes focus on the distance
Your powerful wings
    soar on rising warm currents
    fly through raging storms
Like eagles
    may your nest always be protected
    may you always view the world
            from Olympian heights

July 6, 2002

15

My Companion

A book I never tire of reading
    your smiling face, the intriguing title
    your body language, the enticing synopsis
    the way you wear your clothes, the art on the cover
    the music in your voice, the promise of the prologue
    our goodmorning kiss, the catchy opening to a new
chapter
        your schedule, my schedule
        our together schedule, our unschedule
    your anytimeofday kisses are the little surprises.

Your goodnight kiss turns the chapter's last page of
 a book I never tire of reading.

May 21, 2001 Rev. 9/2/01

My Diamond

Each facet a blue eye
    glowing loving warmth
Blue white light shines
    from inward strength
Strength from crystalline clarity
    softness from a loving touch

July 15, 2005 Rev. 12/27/11 6/8/17

Of Sunshine and Rain

A song sung in morning
flows 'til evening refrain
A song sung in sunshine
changes color in rain

A seed sown in sunshine
bursts open in rain
A seed sown in morning
warms 'til evening refrain

A caress in morning
grows 'til evening refrain
A caress in sunshine
shelters from rain

A life loved in sunshine
weathers well with rain
A life loved in morning
glows 'til evening refrain

Parting

Strong little arms around my neck
Warm little lips against my cheek
Giant sunbeams in a little face
"I love you, Grandpa."

January 2, 1998

Our Inner Garden

Eye holds eye
Word holds word
Soul holds soul
Radiant inner light
Golden essence enfolds us
at ethereal heights
Aroma of jasmine
from our inner garden

Ring holds ring
Vow holds vow
Blessing holds blessing
Aura of the celestial canopy
enlightens
Whispered words
spoken and unspoken
seeds for
our inner garden

Space holds space
Time holds time
Life holds life
Turning world turns our
future
Turning seasons color our inner garden

October 12, 2003 Rev. 10/14/03

Their Music

A cello sings a concerto of life —
heart strings resonate
to a bow drawn by caressing fingers.
The song is harmonized
by a photographer
who sees the world as it is,
yet mounts his camera on angel's wings,
focuses on the world as it should be
and shows us heavenly hues
that picture their music.

Warmth

Through the season of my delight
I bathe in warmth upon my face.
I float with clouds beyond the night

Where heartbeats quicken in the light
Of sandy shores, giant waves and foamy lace
Through the season of my delight.

I photograph this graceful sight
So I'll not forget this place.
I float with clouds beyond the night
Into dreams of wrong and right.

I ask myself,"What is grace
Through the season of my delight?"
My children grown, they now alight
On paths their dreams send them to trace.
I float with clouds beyond the night

Watching as their stars grow bright.
Their love shines warmth upon my face.
Through the season of my delight,
I float with clouds beyond the night.

April 8, 2002

Together

We gave birth to precious sweetness
when our first kisses lingered.
The sweetness a resting place
for body glowing warmth
which bore buds, blossoms, fruit
The sweetness overwhelms summer
seduces winter

Tender kisses linger their taste
on lips
in dreams
Tenderness in touching a cheek
hand holding hand
lips light on finger tips

Sweetness gives joy to our days
Tenderness gives warmth to our nights

August 12, 2004
Rev. 10/08/04; 10/30/04

LIFE & LIVING

Eightieth Birthday

Birthdays cycle through our lives;
we count them as they come.
They multiply before our eyes
into a tidy sum.

But numbers measure quantity,
know nothing about quality
or of our great propensity
for love with much intensity.

So let's count blessings, not the years,
they'll give a tidy sum.
Celebrate each day we live,
not just when birthdays come.

12/31/02

Anniversary Poem

Counting years doesn't help,
nor counting money, either.
When we know how much we've got,
it's time to take a breather.

So breathe with family and your friends:
that's where your value lies.
Your anniversary is an event
we've taken to ritualize.

June 8, 2005

Reflections

A poem is what Life gave to me
A poem of friends and family
A poem to leave my progeny

Each phase a stanza of its own
The world around me set the tone
Each stanza's rhythm stands alone

Life's rising rhythms—surging, churning
Those rising rhythms—growing, learning
Erotic rhythms—youthful, yearning

Then courtship, marriage—rhythm's crest
A boy and girl with rhythms blest
Then rhythms of an empty nest

Awake anew as songbirds sing
To see what life has yet to bring
And travel's rhythms taking wing

The rhythm of our winter years
And keeping step with aging peers
To go where living's rhythm steers

Boy Am I Hip

This hip ain't a hip hooray,
Just want pain to go away.
Doc Bawa said he'd do the job
With saw and drill and gluey glob.
He put in place nice new parts
Using his surgical arts.
A robot was helping him
To place things where space was slim.
Now my leg feels like before --
Maybe just a little sore.
Exercise as I am told —
Don't make moves that are too bold.
Use my walker to be sure
I'm safe while my leg will cure.

January 5, 2022

Bills

Pernicious parasites
arrive on vulture's wings
lay waste our wallets
invoke a fatalistic sigh
counting the pain 'til payday

Bills
Biographical bookmarks
Chapter labels for
needs, pleasures, passions
Index of footnotes
for checkbook literature
Adverbs for activity

Bills
Spots of color
in sweeping swathes
across the living landscape
blend into a pattern
like a painting by Pollack

Bills
Measure of
canyons crossed
mountains climbed
seas sailed
homes built, highways traveled
monuments to self

Bills

No measure of
hands that lift the fallen
comforting ears that listen
laughter with friends
embracing arms that promise
sunny days
star-filled nights

June 22, 2002
Rev. 7/9/02, 8/1/02, 8/7/02

the night wind

lifts a lilting song
in praise of the day's joys
the work well done
chastises failed promise

in my nest
with down of many a year
i cuddle my chicks of happy times
parents romance family career
turn my eggs of unhatched dreams

July 31, 2000

Celebrating One Hundred

A pair of fifties is the theme
Not as old as it may seem
Years ahead have lots in store
Adventures, worries, fun galore
Mind still thinks that you're at prime
Body tells the facts of time
Children give your life some spice
Predictable as tossing dice

What will improve in years ahead:
Slowness with which you move
Need to have your glasses thicken
Less work to make your pulse rate quicken
Forgetting names or what you're doing
Difficulty when you're chewing
Loudness needed for your hearing
Sagging skin that keeps appearing.

"I'll never sound like that!" you said
Until you grew to graying head
Yet, youth did teach to love and care
Qualities your children share
One hundred years has had its day
And what we all would like to say
Two hundred is the goal to set
More happy years are forward yet

May 8, 2009
Rev. 5/6/09, 5/13/09

Cyclist

Wheels bounce 'round hairpin turns
race up a rock-strewn rise
airborne down a sudden slope
Heartbeats pump spinning pedals
Bellows draw the brisk breeze
blow back humid heat
Sweat wets the back
chills the brow
Dust cakes shoes, socks, legs
Dust-caked grin
Bike back in rack
Feet back in sneakers
Engine running
Lower visor against afternoon sun
Shopping list says, "Surprise!"

April 14, 1998

Perfume of Joy

When a refreshing stream
passes through the pasture
of our lives
it nourishes the succulent grasses
that give sustenance
to our souls
It heralds our hearts
to absorb
the perfusive perfume
of joy

September 26, 1999

Our Daughter

A stream
that passes through the pasture
of our life
nourishes the grasses
enriches the clover

She pirouettes
She leaps beyond time and gravity
Her toes twinkle
like a rippling stream in the morning sun

A dance
to the music in the wind
to the song in
her grace
her laugh
her hug

March 3, 1998 Rev. 3/13/98 Rev. 5/12/98

years

flow to the horizon
as clouds cross the sky
roil and rage in turmoil
march in double cadence after a storm
float as feathers on a late day breeze
sanguine wisps in the setting sun
memoirs from sun up to sun down sonnets
beneath the stars

September 29, 2002 Rev. 12/17/02

Discarded

People pass a crumpled, weathered piece
    of paper lying on the street
    sheltered from the turbulent wind
    behind a protruding building entrance.
The piece of paper must have been important —
    to someone
    at some time.
It was carefully made, resolutely used.

How did the wind come to play with it?
    was it carelessly, thoughtlessly tossed?
    did the thrower's aim miss the trash can?
    did the wind mischievously lift it from the trash?
    was it crumpled and tossed in anger, in anguish?

What message did it bring?
    an advertizing offer of service, goods for sale?
    a notice of financial gain or loss?
    a notice of birth or death?
    a vow or disavowal of love?

People pass a crumpled, weathered piece
    of paper lying on the street
    sheltered from the turbulent wind,
    lying next to a crumpled, weathered
        piece of humanity.

May 24, 2001 Rev. 3/19/02

Educator

You taught
Learning is like hiking a steep hill
Find firm footing
Around rocks, over tree roots
Observe everything
      a chipmunk scurrying by
      a woodpecker rat-tat-tatting for food
      a birch tree growing around rocks
Hold these visions
Climb step-by-step
Reach for the top

You taught
Learning is like playing on a rainbow
Test the texture of each color
Savor its flavor
Focus on its fragrance
Hear chromatic harmony
See collected colors synthesize
      into the white light
         of knowledge

You taught
Learning starts with a planted seed
      You gave the water and sunshine

May 28, 2007 Rev. 5/30/07, 6/5/07

Dream Guides

Where are our dreams when we awake?
They are the dawn or our new day.
They are our parasol against the sun,
And our umbrella against the rain.
They are our shopping list for living.
They are the bank book of our deeds.

Our dreams may be abstractions
Of our innermost desires and fears,
But they are also encrypted guides
To what we need from ourselves
To achieve the self-respect
That is the basis of happiness.

July 29, 1995

Life's Essence

I am a still
vaporizing life's substance
condensing the still roiling vapors
into life's essence.

While still tossed
by waves of passion
I row toward what I see
as a still beacon of peace.

Life's substance
includes passion's storms.
Does its essence
seek the stillness of peace?

May 9, 2000

Feelings

Angry I feel like
a rising thermometer
a war drum beating blood to my hands
a bobcat protecting its cubs

Victorious I feel like
a silver-back gorilla pounding his chest
a V-J Day celebration
the echo of a prayer of thanksgiving

Lonely I feel like
a wail in the wilderness
a candle without a flame
an empty pond

Happy I feel like
a prancing squirrel
a child on the last day of school
a colt in spring racing across a meadow

Contented I feel like
a long sip of cappuccino after a gourmet meal
a baby in its mother's arms
a sea lion basking in the sun

April 2004

Friends

The richness in the soil of life.
They hold it firmly
when time's terrible torrents
would wash it away.
They are the rain and sun
that make the soil fertile.

Friends are the reliable tides
that start a ship on its journey
and usher it back to home port.
They are the compass that guides it,
the ballast that gives a stable keel.

Friends are the warmth of a balmy day,
the single shaft of sunlight
that breaks through gloom.
They are extended family —
not born to be,
they chose to be.

Howard

Nice tuh meetcha. I'm Howard.
His smile shy and wary,
brown eyes peek from beneath his eye lids.
He offers a handshake, childlike.
Twenty-three-year-old, five-foot-seven featherweight.

Pvt. Howard Tower,
fires the barracks furnace.
Only a few guys greet him with a smile.
Most ignore him.
A few sneer, Hey, Runt, gonna keep us warm for a
change?
He takes the rudeness quietly.

Over beers at Sally's Bar and Restaurant
outside Fort Eustice, Virginia,
eyes look straight at me,
My mother was proud
when I finished tenth grade and got a job
at the Bijou Theater in Wilkes Barre.
I got to be assistant manager.
I sold tickets, swept between shows,
made the kids behave.
If Al didn't show up,
I ran the projector.
I had lotsa responsibility.

One Wednesday afternoon, he tells me,
I know the guys asked you to go
to the non- com's club.
It's okay.
We can meet next week.
No, I reply, I'll see them another time.
That night, relaxed after a beer, he muses,

Tom's really a good guy,
but he looks down on anyone
who ain't as smart as him.
Dick's smart, but ain't got no confidence.
Depends on others too much.
Jack always smiles and spits lies through his
smiling teeth.
You know, Charlie really ain't as smart as he tries
to make you think.
Yeah, they tease and play tricks on me because
I ain't so smart.
So I stay out of their way.
They ain't bad, just don't know no better.

What would the world be like
if its smart guys had Howard's smarts?

October 20, 1998
Rev. November 20, 1998

The Bull and Thrush

The bull snorted and pawed the ground
at any movement of the cape of criticism.
He bellowed loudly,
"You don't know what you are talking about!"
He charged with his sharp verbal horns
to gore the cape before it moved again.
Then the thrush would sing, sharply at first, then more scftly
and rhythmically.
The bull would breathe more slowly,
and, inhaling the flowers,
would again be Ferdinand.

Bare Windows

Sun peers through a bare window
Cheerful rays feel the chill of emptiness
Gone the toddler grown to woman
     left for college
     left home
Gone the bed, books, desk, dresser
Gone the sound of her smile

Another window
Gone the little boy grown to man
     left for college
     left home
Gone the bed, desk, beer bottle collection
the dresser earned by a month's neatness
Gone the warmth of teasing

Emptiness again
where a young couple shared love
nurtured children
     sent them to college
     set them free
Gone their portraits
     from wedding
     to recent anniversary
Gone pictures of a prior generation
Gone their tears and laughter

Sun follows across a continent
peers through a window
Finds familiar pictures
Its cheerful rays feel the warmth of
 the once young couple
visited by children, grandchildren

September 24, 2007

Chocolate Cream Pie

dessert fork
firmly surrounded
by slender fingers

cutting edge down
forefinger presses
steadily

across the point
of the freshly cut
portion

through cream
through chocolate
through crust

fork turns
pinky
poised

scoops up
severed
morsel

lifts to
waiting
mouth

lips close
eyes close
curl into smile

August 18, 2005

Footsteps of Time

Time walks
quietly on a country road
noisily on a city street
in moccasins along
a pristine woodland trail
It carries our heartbeats
orchestrates our
breathing in
breathing out
our sleeping, waking

Count its footsteps in
growing gold of sunrises
crimson sunsets
body-warmed beds made
cups of body-warming coffee
empty cereal boxes
rolls of toilet paper

Count its miles in
babies first healthy cry
first tentative steps
worried first day of school
joy of high school graduation
proud college degree
happy, tearful wedding
glory of grandchild
new headstones in cemetery

Jan. 31, 2009 Rev. 02/21/09

A Great Depression Morning

Damn you, sun, don't speed from sleep to shine.
Let me lie warm in memories
of clients waiting for my counsel,
of cleverly applied precedent of law
that rewarded my client in court
who handsomely rewarded me,
of ample fare for family, help for friends
 before my partner cheated me
and we broke up in thirty-three.

Don't rush me into today
when I must search for work,
carry another client through bankruptcy,
extend my palm to family for help
to pay rent, buy shoes, buy food.
Does economy commit tort
that I can charge in court?
I could plead a woeful wrong
done my wife and heirs.
But what defendant can I charge
with cheating people of life that's theirs,
of making people live with fear
they won't survive another year?
Now I have to play my part
burdened by a heavy heart.

Damn you, sun, don't speed from sleep to shine.

February 4, 2001 Rev. 3/4/01, 4/?/01

41

Heritage

Our roots hold life's earth firm
      beneath our feet
give our souls strength
      against savage storm
warn us, if we listen,
      of tainted soil

They store our strength
      spread early into learning
absorb ideas and faith
      implant them into our every fiber

Our roots grow when
      our minds are nourished
nourished by the soil
      of heritage

Nov. 11, 2007

Living Fabric

I weave fabric from my life
denim for cooking, cleaning, carpentry
sackcloth for sorrows
cushioned cotton for baby care
velvet for the luxury of leisure

Figures form in texture and colors
sculptured by sewn contours
A prince on white steed
       kisses awake a dainty damsel
A maiden fair finds beauty in a beast
A baby rocks in a tree top
All come alive
in the fabric of my life

December 8, 1998
Rev. December 30, 1998

The Light In The Window

Will it be there whenever I return
Its warmth hides the dark
Will it carpet my steps to the door
Look into eyes
      that shine into mine
Will it surround the table set
      with flowers
      steaming roast
         on china platter

Will it be there whenever I return

February 14, 2005 Rev. 4/13/05

Remembering a Valiant Life

Wake to
sunshine of a smile
smile of sunshine
voice of living song
song of a loving voice
warmth of human touch
touch of human warmth

Read books
Explore — challenge ideas.
Share brightness among the stars
with people on symbiotic orbits.

Wait to be lifted
from bed to wheelchair.
Wheelchair stroll,
greet neighbors.
"I'm fine. Thanks for asking.
"But are you over your cold?
"And your mother,
"is she still in the hospital?"

"Thanks for taking me to get my nails done.
"Now I'll check my e-mail.
I expect several replies."

Inside looking out
disregard skin stretched
over sinking frame.
See throb of living,
hear living song.

Heartbeat is rhythm,
art-of-living provides music,
love and the joy of loving
write the words.

February 26, 2007
Rev. 2/28/07, 3/2/07, 3/5/07, 3/6/07, 3/13/07

Little Hands, Eyes, Feet

A new hand reaches for tomorrow
A pink little hand
with fingers tightly curled
around the bell cord of the future.

A tiny fist searches for a mouth
that wants the taste of mother's breast —
nourishment from the world today
for strength in a world yet to be.

Small, searching eyes follow a new light.
A light that is a beacon of dreams,
that warns of rocks and shallows,
that shines on promise.

Baby feet kick the air today
grow to walk firmly into untrod time.

Memories

A supple place
guards sleeping memories of
       childhood
       youth
       marriage
       growing children

Memories sleep with
silver strings tied to toes
until a fleeting flash
sparked in slumber
tugs a string

Some memories wake
excited, capricious
mix with funky facts
       naked in Macy's
       horses pass speedy Corvette

Some annoyed at arousal
envelop fears
       turn friends into fiends
       vehicles into monsters
       spring rain into level 5
           hurricane

Others wake with stretch and smile
don't redress the mind with guile
refine reflections to harmony
start day in peaceful litany

Memories —
molds from metered time
wait for our hearts
to pour lead, silver, gold

Tamed
they buoy
our earthly feet
into tomorrow

September 23, 2006

The Hole

Unlike a hole in sand
        soon filled by tide's ebb and flow
a hole gouged from embracing arms
        lasts
Walk in a wilted garden
        under a black sun sky
a void devoid of light

Silent voices of embracing faces
        sing of love beams reaching
to float the empty soul
        above the black air of the hole
Again to see the smiling golden sun
        and see in its smile
the happy memories
        that live on in the heart.

July 27, 2005
Rev. 9/26/05, Oct. '05, 1/25/11, 8/20/15, 2/10/16

Reaching

I reached far up
 pulled down a sheet of sky
  made a majestic mantle
   found Knowledge

I reached out
 scooped up brilliant light
  poured it into a crystal bowl
   found Understanding

I reached to a black cloud
 grasped a lightening bolt
  made a crown for my head
   found Imagination

I reached high
 put a leash on a white billowy cloud
  taught it to heel, stay, sit
   found Discipline

I reached beyond the shore
 held an ocean wave in my arms
  taught it to carry me over obstacles
   found Ambition

I wrapped my arms around a mountain
 unrolled its rocky peak
  let it lift my mind
   found Perspective

I reach beyond inside myself
 moved by dreams of glowing sunrise
  seek the source of cosmic light
   reaching for Purpose

November 10, 2005 Rev. 11/19/05, 11/27/05

Warmth
(A Villanelle)

Through the season of my delight
I bathe in warmth upon my face.
I float with clouds beyond the night

Where heartbeats quicken in the light
Of sandy shores, giant waves and foamy lace
Through the season of my delight.

I photograph this graceful sight
So I'll not forget this place.
I float with clouds beyond the night

Into dreams of wrong and right.
I ask myself,"What is grace
Through the season of my delight?"

My children grown, they now alight
On paths their dreams send them to trace.
I float with clouds beyond the night

Watching as their stars grow bright.
Their love shines warmth upon my face.
Through the season of my delight,
I float with clouds beyond the night.

April 8, 2002

Resolution

I resolve to be a better me
not to arbitrarily disagree
nor gorge on every food I see

I've got to lose my portly gain
reduce my heavy cardiac strain
take less in stomach — more in brain

I have to lower cholesterol
also reduce my alcohol
walk outside or in the mall

I have to learn to keep my cool
so I won't sound a blasted fool
dripping words from caustic pool

I'll give my wife much more respect
not deny her intellect
and, sometimes, tell her she's correct

My family has to have first place
above business, ball game or a race
spend more time being face-to-face

Resolutions add each New Year's Day
don't seem to do the things I say
it's a portrait of me like Dorian Gray

February 7, 2004

Inner Worlds

I have worlds within me
circling my dreams
radiance illumines
warmth nurtures

Warm worlds
peopled with
sights, sounds, sensations
rained on with ideas
that write themselves

Oh, orbiting moons,
don't eclipse my dreams.
don't give day darkness,
but reflect into darkness
some light.

October 25, 2003
Rev. 11/17/03, 1/3/04

Snow Satan's Blessing

Sooty city of yesterday
coated deep in swan's down
Buildings, fire hydrants
wear fluffy white hats
windows wear white mustaches
mud-spattered cars
become smooth sculptures
A primal scene for
poets, painters, musicians
for ski slopes, ski shops

The rattling rush
of the bladed behemoth
tosses alabaster clouds
conceals cars
Autos hush along the road
pack the unskimmed layer
headlights play on glistening glaze
tail lights glow like cherry stains
Rumbling salt trucks, sand trucks
spread their stuff

Shovels clatter, scrape
unbury walks, autos
overtax hearts
We clamber across uncleared walks
slowly assail slippery surfaces
broken bone falls on ice
Time changes white to
gray, brown, black

Listen to the beauty of
pristine promises
Live with delivered reality

January 29, 2004

Mountain Mood

See the freedom of
      a soaring hawk
      soft floating clouds
          white and lavender grey
      lichen on fir tree trunks
      sharp green needles on branches
Feel the softness of
      moist earth
      squooshiness of mud
      treachery of loose gravel
      cleansing wash of mountain breeze
          on cheeks
Fill lungs with
      scent of moist brown birch leaves
      aroma of fir trees
Hear silence
      now and then interrupted by
      rustling of scurrying rodent or rabbit
      rat-a-tat-tat of a red crested wood pecker
          searching for a meal
      hum of a breeze through birch and fir
Taste your oneness with nature

October 10, 2005

Regeneration

Old muscles become
       stories told in mirth
Brain cells wander, hide, tease
Remind me where to go
       not what to do there
Words as pictures parade
       on a steamed window of memory

Past vigor sews new life
       nourishes new growth
       yields new ideas
Reminders of
       the fruitful fragrance of youth
       the teacher of my visions

February 22, 2005
Rev. 3/1/05, 4/16/05, 5/17/05

Music Moves

Music measures the moving world
the rhythm among stars
the twinkling lights of fireflies
the call of birds
the beating heart
the drum roll bringing rain

Music moves the spinning mass
the life forms from its womb
swaying flora beneath the sea
grass on breezy plains
air soaked deep into lungs
water through fish's gills

Music molds the human mind
sets rhythm for the thoughts
crickets chirping on a summer's eve
an orchestra playing a Viennese waltz
a newscaster's staccato report
a lone bugler sounding Taps
at soldiers' freshly filled graves

December 26, 2003 Rev. 1/6/04

Octogenarian

Eighty is a lot of years;
you wonder where they went.
Look around and it appears
it wasn't just an accident.
Yesterday as just a tad,
you'd wend your way home from school
and show your grades to Mom and Dad.
As years went by you wondered who'll
want to make her home with you.
You found that special girl of yours
who made your dream come true.
You had a home and many chores,
kept important things in sight.
You had a share of happy times;
family grew to your delight.
The years have rung their many chimes.
This year tolls full eighty.
We wish you health in years ahead;
we wish they're not too weighty
and love should keep your heart well fed.

September 4, 1997

When I say Kaddish —

I speak to them:
to Marilyn, my wife
    Who shared my life and bore our children;
to Dad
    who taught philosophy, baseball and courage;
to sister Doris,
    who mothered her little brother,
    and went to college proms with him
    when he couldn't get a date,
to Grandma Jenny
    who always gave me a second portion at dinner;
to Grandpa Frank
    after whom I am named
    a gentle man I wish I had known;
to Grandma Edith
    who died when I was too young to remember;
to Grandpa Hirsch
    who cried when my mother sang Eli-Eli;
to the aunts and uncles who enriched my life
    with their love and caring.
I speak to them in my heart —
and their love answers me.

The Moving Clock

Morning
Sightless seeing unsees it all
The moving clock behind the wall
The turning world his eyes don't see
His time as growing like a tree
With fragrant buds he does not smell
Sweet fruit ripens
                    untouched lonely sentinel
Plucked by any hands that come along
While business bee makes honey
                    to his buzzing song
Works the hive from dawn to dusk
His treatment of detractors
                    brusque
But then the turning world turns hair to gray
He sees the clock behind the wall
Where went noon?
                    Where went day?
Where the fruit from my tree grown tall?
My honey pot is full
                    How can that be all?

May 14, 2003
Rev. 5/19/03, 5/27/03

59

Senior Moments

Fine thoughts I think escape my mind.
I frustrate at the void that's left behind.
These wondrous thoughts I would express
when I have someone to impress.

I should write them down like schoolboy cheating
and save them for a social meeting.
I'd sneak a peek while others speak
and wait my chance to give some cheek.

Those who hear would surely gasp
to hear the depth of thought I grasp.
They'd look at me with great respect
admiring such sharp intellect.

They'd ask my thoughts on many topics,
smart investing, rainforests in the tropics.
I'd illustrate financial planning,
how satellites do IR scanning

To measure how much waste we've gained
and how we're ecologically strained,
how tribal greed in world affairs
sends social progress down the stairs
to Hades, how partisan political votes
prevent what right reason promotes.

Life has changed since I was young,
and now my memory's unstrung.
Important facts I can't recall —
names, dates, places and all.

If you would ask me what I think,
I'd smile and give a happy wink
and tell a tale from years way back
I'd hope would fit the questions's track.

February 21, 2000 Rev. 3/?/00

The Old Family Car
When time and miles tolled the death knell,
the cylinders of our '65 Dodge Coronet station wagon
    gasped their last.
Yesterday, its winter primping — plugs, points, timing.
Our daughter's first lesson in auto mechanics.
Perfectly done, but the engine
    won't sing, sputter or cough.
An hour of checking contacts, checking dwell,
    checking timing — nothing.
Tow to mechanic, "No compression," he says.

It's memorial, our memories:
children's grade school to grad school
a suitcase on wheels for
    a summer month in New Hampshire
    a year on college campus
    Nana and Zaida to their bungalow.

We know the car had soul.
It gave it's all to us.

May 14, 2003

The Checkbook

A checkbook is a useful thing.
A ledger of one's living.
Debits minus, credits add;
simple math — that's not so bad.
I was good at calculus,
so checkbooks shouldn't be a fuss.
But they seem to have their tricks
 that question three and three are six.

The checkbook checks 100 low.
Where the hell did that much go?
Ah! The check to Joe two months ago
 those two statements still don't show.
Okay, now the check book is 40 high.
So where did things go awry?

Proceed along each iteration
accompanied by consternation.
This monthly ill gone loudly sonic
is finally cured by vodka tonic.

September 10, 2012 Rev.9/25/21

Time Flow

Hear time
flow
on notes of native flute
Sound of days
melting into memory
with drum-beat rhythm

Life — a river of time
seeded by mountain rain —
roils around rocks
placid through flowering meadows
reaches its end in infinite sea
Warmed by spirit sun
chilled by mountain breeze
starts its journey anew

Spirit song in the heart
sails upstream
along life's river
through cycles of seasons
listens to bygone souls
speak in the breath of a flute

July 18, 2008
Rev. 8/16/08

Wheeling

I started out in morning dew.
and traveled an uncharted way
through desert, forest, fields of hay,
judging when to leave and when to stay,
to meet someone I wished I knew.

I turned at Wayward Cross one day,
wheeled beside a gorgeous blonde.
No dust was strewn by fairy wand.
We parted down at Lonesome Pond —
the blonde just bade me go my way.

A man wheeled by, said,"Howdy son.
You're okay, your wheels still turn,
and I can see your young pants burn."
He knew he'd made my stomach churn;
my red face his food for fun.

I let the wind howl through my hair,
fan my face, cool my mind;
his joke about my pants unkind
showed that people aren't blind..
I knew I'd entered mid-day's lair

when an angel joined my jaunty ride,
held my hand, searched my eyes,
coyly let me think I'm wise.
I knew whole love without disguise —
floated on a rising tide.

Soon enough our wheels bore more.
A girl and boy were our reward
for hills we'd climb and streams we'd ford.
These blossomed beauties we adored.
Their wheels soon spun as ours before.

Now the late day sun has glowed.
Young wheels have wheeled their hopeful ways;
we watch them go with pride and praise.
We've slowed our wheels in this late phase
with no refueling on this road.

August 7, 1999
Rev. 8/15/99, 10/18/99, 11/15/99, 11/20/99, 3/5/00

Timeless Time

A line of time
ranges to the edge of the universe
where the past
      is the present
           is the future
finds its own beginning
whirls with it through the firmament
as a song
      heard by living energy
surrounds galaxies
      passes through atoms

Living energy
a life-force beyond life
a blower of breath through life's flute
      from infant's cry
           to spirit's rising sigh
a singer of songs sensed
not heard
songs of lights
      beacons
           wings in the wind
songs from earth's soul

Time is a coupler of visions
visions seen from beyond space
      crafted in music
      telling the untellable
a carrier of dreams
from generations ahead
      to those behind
         and back again

Time is timeless
      around us
in light from sun and stars
in sounds of
      people
      birds
      wind
      breath of a flute

January 1, 2008 Rev. 5/3/08

White Water

Insects ride a leaf
caught in a careening current
Irrational, over-reactive, chaotic forces
push them through highs and stomach-churning lows
like unstable stock prices on a demented day
Rush them past turkey vultures
that feed on a crushed carcass
a young bear who chanced a weak footing
fished, and overextended its reach to make a kill
Eager eddies suck in the helpless
Squirrels collect their acorns
The roar of the white turbulence drowns
the song of mockingbird, caw of crow
musical hush of willow, growl and groan of oak

"Rocks ahead!"
"Hard right paddles! Harder! HARDER!!"
Wet with sweat and spray
Hang over to keep from flipping
Swoosh
"YEEEHAAA!"
A grazing deer startled
watches

"Waterfall!"
"HOLD TIGHT!"
Knuckles bleach white
Trees swirl past SLAM, SPLASH
 paddle

Pull up on a calm shore
Count arms, legs, bruises
Recount tactics, traumas, thrills
after a day on Wall Street

October 9, 1997 Rev. 12/4/97

Your Reflection

Learn from mirror faces you meet.
 Do they show a welcome shine,
cast a cloudy gloom?
Learn, too, if you truly see you,
or an image bent by ill intent.

Piece together a mosaic
from a myriad of mirrors large and small,
above and below, to right and left.
Mirrors silvered by family, friends, strangers
by different race, religion, sex.
Follow the patterns you see.
Judge these glasses for clarity
images for disparity.

November 6, 1998
Rev. December 20, 1998

GROWING

A Baby Grows

One year, one year, one year old;
That's how old I am, I'm told.
Two feet, two feet, two feet tall;
That's my mark upon the wall.
Walking, walking by myself;
Soon I'll reach up to the shelf.
Kisses, kisses, hug and hold —
One year, one year, one year old.

Two years, two years, two years old.
My verbal skills will now unfold.
Books to read and lots of toys
Are among my greatest joys.
My mommy and my daddy dear
Give me love and lots of cheer.
Growing bright and growing bold —
Two years, two years, two years old.

Feb. 3, 1996

Above the Haze

The mountain's peak is out of view above the haze,
but its base is firmly planted.
The water in its streams have unfamiliar clarity,
a simple, uncomprehensible purity.

Climb,
Stumble on loose rocks;
slip on gravel and mud.
Roots and branches reach out support, prevent
back-sliding,
become your Jacob's ladder.
Rest on soft grass
beneath a wizened oak.
Nearby a crystalline spring serves refreshment
from between mossy rocks.
It cools the head, calms the spirit.
Focus returns to the beckoning trail.

Now, friends with the mountain,
feel its spirit.
Climb with steady, strenuous strides.
At the height of the climb,
become one
with the surrounding freshness and peace.
See above and beyond the haze
which, after all, had only been in the mind.

7/12/82
Revs.: 6/22/97
7/22/97

Chided Child

Please rub my sore no more.
It's been rubbed raw to my core.
Chides in childhood gnaw and gnaw;
 'till I can't rid them from my craw.
Is respectful silence a fateful flaw?

The ribald chides demean my pride,
force my dignity aside.
Happy times unhappily belied.
I wash the sore with brackish tide
of tears I hold and learn to hide.

April 22, 2002 Rev. 5/28/02; 9/30/02

Flowers of War

Fields tilled by mines, mortars, bombs
harrowed by tank treads
pain planted with bayonets
fed with blood
Gnarled scaly stalks push through the rage
watered by rain of bullets
buds bloom glistening glacial white
hide from lightning, savage storm
vainly seek solace from sun
We harvest
        battered blooms of youth
        hungry flowers with
        sad sagging petals
        nectar of burning tears

September 30, 2002
Rev. 11/19/02, 11/21/02, 11/22/02, 2/2/16,7/27/22

73

Reader

Butterfly eyes flit page to page,
pollinate dreams and understanding,
sip rich cerebral nectar,
make jewels of verbal dew drops
on precious mental petals.

Finding a flower's nectar spent,
butterfly eyes, not yet content,
fly on a gentle breeze of thought
to another sun soaked flower —
fly to a symphony of words
threaded with their own rhythm.
Rhythm moving with meaning;
meaning woven in words,
words sweet as nectar.

August 11, 1999 Rev.11/15/99, 3/5/00

Voices

A whisper stands on my shoulders
fills my ears with its hushed voice,
a voice that is the voices
of those I love, who love me,
of those who taught me.

The whisper stands heavily on my shoulders.
I shout, "Hush up!" "Go a way!" "Shoo, shoo!"
but it has filled me with its words.
Grating words replay and replay
as a looped audio tape.

Oh no! The voice includes mine
from some unearthly place in time
saying, "Your choice now foretells how you will
be known when honor alone
sets your path through unmarked byways."

Can I still my own voice when it tells me I've no
one else to blame?

January 27, 2003
Rev. 2/21/03, 3/28/03, 5/11/03

TRAVEL

Argentine Tango

Step — step — slide, slide, slide
Toy with your partner
match stride for stride
Draw him, coax him
tether him taut
Poles to the tension
dancers have wrought
harmony, drama
Heads upward flick
legs intertwine
courtingly kick
Glide to the rhythm
slow — slow — quick, quick, quick

May 3, 1998

Solitude At Sea

I watch ultramarine sea
move to wind's mood.
Ripples ride waves,
White wisps splash tips.

Our keel intrudes on a world
of grouper, swordfish, squid, shark;
of sea fan, sponge, starfish.
A world of quiet rhythm.

We roll to the rhythm,
Weave a wake of turquoise froth.
Warm in late day sun,
Cross a boulevard of rippling gold.

Li Jiang*
(Clear River)

Clear Water
liltingly whispers its entry,
oozes from rain soaked earth
gurgles from springs
        like a dance on a xylophone,
sings with rippling voice
        from rushing streams,
 roars with tympanic crescendo
        in water falls
makes harmonious chorus
        with the timeless
        song of the river
through gorges and calm depths.

Softly swaying to the rhythm
        of river's song,
sweet green grass,
fanned pheasant-tail bamboo,
weeping willows
leisurely sip
        the clear green water.
Carp, catfish, trout
feed, mate, move
        with the melody.
Green-haired granite monoliths
rise like orchestral musicians
        above the Clear River,
white veiled in the mystery
        of morning mist,
make their music
        to guard against evil spirits.

River people know the song
        the music in their voices,
        a dance in their step.
One fisherman walks a tread-wheel
        to hoist his net
        on the crane at the bow
        of his bamboo raft.
Another fisherman's trained cormorant
        dives, returns
        with a ten-inch carp.
Squatting women
        dip clothes in the river,
        beat them on rocks,
        ring them,
        gossip.
Children run along the shore,
        net for shrimp,
        swim,
        dive for coins thrown by tourists.

Clear River sings the people's song,
        flows into timeless time.

* Li Jiang (Chinese for "Clear River") flows past Guilin, China

June 23, 2001 Rev. 8/24/01

Milford Sound, New Zealand

Jagged steep sides of brush-bearded rock
slice into the glacier-gouged fjord
from glacier-glazed, cloud-capped peaks.
Random rays peak through blue holes,
glisten on thousand-foot cascading silver streams,
streams that crash onto fallen dark rocks,
churn into turquoise sea.

Porpoises ply the waters for snapper, krill, cod;
broach the surface, spout, arch through the air.
Sated fur seals snooze on flat stone slabs.
Fishermen, sailers, power craft cruise the choppy surface.
Water skiers side-slide, zig-zag, jump the wake.

I view nature's majestic beauty and power
and see my light
as a firefly in the milky way.

January 29, 2000

Sailing the Storm

The captain steers his course as told
the compass is ignored.
His helmsman lauds him for calm seas.
The captain listens — bored.

Storm arises, attacks the ship
with roiling roll of raging sea.
The captain in his glory now
repeats his orders happily.

He shouts how he will save the ship
and steers her with the wind.
He says the trouble is the fault
of all of those who'd sinned.

He fuels the engines, gains more speed.
Detractors have no sway.
The Lord has told him what to do.
The Lord he would obey.

He sees he'd not outrun the storm,
 turns the ship around.
Says this is the way for us to win.
Safe harbor would be found.

He says he'd not run out of fuel,
of that he'd been assured.
By using more and speeding up
all problems would be cured.

The crew is busy down below;
 the bilge is being pumped.
Passengers are angry now —
want the crew be dumped.

The captain loudly praises them,
his faith is in their deeds.
He says he surely understands
the problems and their needs.

The purser wires for fuel.supply
He'll pay with IOU's.
The sources who will hold the notes
could call them when they'd choose.

The captain says our credit's good;
the debt will help our business.
He sails the ship without a thought
of future fiscal illness.

May 1, 2006 Rev. 5/2/06

Sicilian Memory

The Land
Vulcan voiced volcanic roars
Heaved land above the sea
Lava flowed down to the shores
Monoliths rose to prominency

Ceres filled the fertile land
Farmers found it good to use
Trees, grain, flowers on every hand
Muses formed artistic views

The Experience
Friendly smiles everywhere
Buon Girono, Buena Serra
Pizzeria, Tratoria — one here, one there
Ruins from Greek and Roman era

Winged chariots brought us here
To roam this land with new fair friends
We've laughed and aah'd — and now a tear
 But the memory never ends

May 11, 2007

Sicilian Recipe

In a large stew pot
      bottom lightly coated with Prehistory
add Iberian, Phoenician, Trojan
Stir gently
Add Greek
Let stand until reaction starts
Beat violently until steaming stops
Let simmer in its own warmth until cool
Add Roman and repeat process
      - beating is quicker and cooling, longer
Season lightly with Barbarian
Stir in Saracen in removable pieces
Let soak
Add Norman, which removes Saracen
      leaving some remnants
Flavor lightly with German, English
      Garnish with a touch of American
Sicilian is ready
Flavor variations from morsel to morsel
      enhance the experience

May 11, 2007

Soho

Streets are bright, art is the mood
Painting, sculpture, fashion, food
Talents contrive to breathe art alive
Gentrified slum — old tree, fresh plum

Lamb laced on skewers, pints from the brewers
Tongue tingling curry, Big Mac for a hurry
Veal scallopini served on linguini
Mixed veggies roasted, garlic bread toasted
Primavera fucilli, jalapeno chili
Sea food au gratin — oops, Rolaids forgotten

Living goddesses strut with a flair
Enticing exposure shows what they dare
Molded in satin or ruffled like Latin
Red skirted hips with bright matching lips
Evening attire with sparkling crown
Gracefully flowing bridal gown

Art of all manner from chisel and hammer
Smooth oaken shapes, bright paper crepes
Brush and paint both abstract and quaint
Lifelike statues sitting in chairs
Accurate down to the soft pubic hairs
Wall mounted figures reach out in relief
With happy bright colors or shaded in grief

Painting, sculpture, fashion, food
Streets are bright, art is the mood

April 11, 2000; Rev. 4/17/00, 5/15/00

The Rhine River

What wisdom has the Rhine River
learned all these eons

I who live by physical laws
do not need wisdom
Wisdom is for you who live
by social laws
who must decide between
kindness and selfishness
friend and foe

The Waking Dragon

A bamboo flute dances my wings to China
      like a butterfly drawn to a lotus blossom
to hear the music of their voices
      the rhythm of their lives.

      The People
A Guilin farmer carries his weight of bok choy
      balanced on a bamboo pole;
his wife hoes the field, carries her weight in river water
      to their hilltop home.
A Danang River fisherman walks his sampan's tread wheel
      hoisting his net,
his wife farms, scrubs clothes in the river.
A Wuchow worker lays bricks or porters a payload;
his wife sweeps streets or cooks stir-fry at a sidewalk eatery.
A Shanghai professor teaches top-scoring students
his wife gleans financial facts from her office computer.

      The Politics
Near the Great Wall of ideology
      look for the watchman's fire
      listen for his horn
warning against invading hordes
      of feudal past
      of a modern plotical future.
Chin, Tong, Ming, Ching Dynasties
      ravaged by human storm
      washed into history
      woven into the nest
of the waking, hungry dragon.

November 6, 2000

NATURE

A Grain of Time Suspended

 Earth
Sleepy sun snuggles into bed.
Misty breath of her drowsy yawn
closes the rose, lifts robin's wings to nest,
draws the deer to evening drink,
lulls the wind to rest,
wakes the frog to chorus,
the firefly to fairy games,
the horned owl to hunt.

 Heavens
The glow from sun's drowsy eye
colors cumulus clouds pink and purple
against a blue white sky.
Her eye quickly closes;
her last limb is tucked from sight.
Twinkling dots draw imaginary pictures.
Night's lantern bathes Earth in silvery white light.

 Lovers
Sitting, side pressed to side
arms around waists
heads tilted to touching,
man and woman enfold the song of solitude,
embrace the intimacy of darkness.
Moonglow eyes sparkle replies to fireflies.

August 5, 2000
Rev. 11/7/00, 11/?/00, 8/18/02; 4/24/06

A River . . .

flows like thoughts through my mind
glistens in morning sun
shimmers as a dew strewn meadow
      in morning breeze
stormy fast water roiling
      around rocks
seductive in a quiet cove
      shaded by gold green willows
      with soft moss on the bank

A River . . .
source of sustenance
flows through distance as I through time
slows in the deep, mature bed
gives to those who depend on it
until it reaches land's end

February 1, 2005
Rev. 02/22/2005, 5/04/05

A Summer Saga

Noontime shadows grown short.
Fields of corn, wheat, oats enrich horizons,
press thirsty mouths to earth that asks for rain.

A sudden cool wind whips dust, lofts debris, lifts skirts.
Like a herald trumpeting arriving royalty,

The low roll of thunder announces nature's power.
Dark, roiling clouds flash their energy;
blue-white spears pierce into earth, roar defiance.

Earth drinks its fill. Rivulets run
from the corners of its mouth.
In an hour, sun cheers birds to song, the young to play,

Men and women to work, the old to the joy of warmth.
Fair skin, bared by string bikinis
laid out to worship solar radiance.

Laid out to radiate on worshiping watchers.

April 21, 2002, Rev. 9/30/02, 7/1/23

As Time Sails

The ship's prow plows untouched time
securing space for NOW
Astern — time already lived —
playfully closes behind NOW
sweeps forcefully into memory
looking like a swept path
to the horizon of recollection
where sun rose
and now lights living world
along its arc to time's end

December 14, 2009

A Titan's Tantrum

Fire in its belly
Earth rages
Heavy hobnailed boot
kicks Sea solidly in the seat
Sea roils — rises
Throws a mighty fist into Earth's face
Tears away covering green
Swallows land
Piles debris, human and flora
Buries in mud
Washes other remains into the ocean
Leaves salted earth dead
Poisons fresh water with salt

The Titans become quiet
Sun weeps on the scene
Feet again move about
Hands dig with hope
Love searches for loved ones
          mourns the lost
Disaster becomes
a source of humanity

The Titans — the source
          of life
          of death

February 27, 2005

93

At the Lake

Grey bars imprison a crimson face
whose rays slice
the darkening velvet blue sky
with scarlet stripes,
reflect on rippling water
like dancing rose petals.
The breeze stops to rest
among the leaves.
Pine, ash, oak sharply outline
against a red and gold horizon.
A frog croaks greeting —
answers echo back from among the lily pads.
A bass leaps, catches a fly.
Rippling circles
reflect sunset blue, red, gold
swim for the farthest shore.
Tired, they are no more.

April 14, 1998

Golden Light

Morning squints open its golden eye.
Golden light guilds the tip
of the centennial elm
on top of Cemetery Hill,
climbs down the tree,
down the hill,
walks into town.

March 29, 2003 Rev. 9/1/03

December

Aging Autumn
flexes waning muscle
ground warming sun
frost coating chill
snow, sleet, rain
ground warming sun

Aging Autumn entertains infant Winter
whips naked trees to groaning
cherry-pinches noses, cheeks
billows debris aloft
resettling the landscape
lashes wind-howled rain along the street
punches leaning people, wetting feet

Child Winter laughs a frigid laugh
freezes Autumn's rain
forms cloud yielding droplets
into frosty hexametric feathers
dusts trees, houses alabaster
coats the land for sleighs and plows
snowmen and forts

Autumn smiles a wrinkled smile
retires with winter solstice
As with politicians
Winter harvests energy
from the year's dark days
and blows a blinding storm

January 30, 2004

Evening

The sleepy sun snuggles into bed.
The musty breath of its drowsy yawn
closes the rose, lifts robin's wings to nest,
 draws the deer to evening drink,
lulls the wind to rest,
wakes the frog to chorus,
the firefly to fairy games,
the horned owl to hunt.

The glow from sun's drowsy eyes
colors cumulus clouds in pink and purple
against a blue white sky.
These eyes quickly close.
Twinkling points of light
draw imaginary pictures —
Libra, Leo, Orion,
Scorpio, Cassiopeia, Pleiades.
Earth bathes in silvery white light.

Admiring the evolution
side pressed to side
arms around waists
heads tilted to touching,
they enfold the song of solitude,
embrace the privacy of darkness.
Misty eyes sparkle replies to fireflies.
A grain of time stays
suspended in the hourglass.

July 31, 2000

Clouds

Shapeless vessels float on an invisible sea. Towering
pillars grasp the first light of day.
Quiet puffs golden in the morning sun.
A landscape molded by the whims of sun and wind
that may be blown apart and reshaped
and again be peaceful before day's end.
All are moving shadows between sunrise and sunset
    and quiet ghosts beneath the stars.

November 14, 1983
Rev. 9/29/96, 2/21/98, 9/9/15
Written to Mom (in the hospital after her accident) while flying on a business trip.

Farewell Song

What song are the birds singing?
It isn't their usual welcome to the first golden ray
    sparkling on dew-crusted gardens.
Ahh, it is their autumn farewell song.
Cardinal, robin, finch embrace their neighbors
sing forwarding address for southern homes.
Starling, sparrow, crow answer in harmony
    wishing them
    good voyage, pleasant winter, safe return.
They fuel for flight from the plentitude of autumn-
ripened seeds, loam-nourished worms,
sing prayers of thanks for the bounty,
leave as trees change from green finery
    to yellow, orange, red
    before donning gray winter nightgowns.
I wave them adieu.
They dip a wing and sing,
    "Come! We've room for you, too!"

October 8, 2001
Rev. 11/27/01, 12/03/01

February

I greet February with a shiver
     and a cup of hot tea
with boots, shovel, snow melt
emergency generator ready to roar
I'm not of the snow birds swarming to
     Florida, Arizona, Southern Cal
No Carribean cruise or flight to Cancun
Just a wind-frozen macho smile
     at the myth of being rugged
Hmmm, symptom of diminished-daylight doldrums

Time for diversion by celebration
A salute to the warmth of a smile
heart-flowered sentiment, flowers, candy,
phone calls to dear ones
Salutes to Washington who liberated
     Thirteen Colonies
to Lincoln who liberated Slaves
to Reagan who liberated Conservatives
A salute to the wane of Winter
     who can save a blizzardly blast
     'til Ides of March goes past

February 9, 2004
Rev. 02/21/04, 2/26/04, 3/22/04

98

Fireflies

The last limb of the sun has folded behind the hills,
which are sharply outlined against a cobalt sky.
The meadow is a blackish green dotted white
where daisies pick up the last light from the sky.
The twinkling neighbors around Venus haven't awakened yet,
but, in the east, Neptune and Saturn
are surrounded by their company of sparkling jewels.
A lone cricket sets the orchestral key;
one by one the myriad instruments repeat the note.
Their minstrelsy soon envelopes the air.

A greenish-white flash appears in the meadow.
To the left a blinking light answers, then one to the right.
Soon, like a luminous fountain, flashing lights dance
and harmonize with the cricket orchestra.
The moon is not yet awake, and the stars and fireflies
are choruses in counterpoint.
As the night darkens, these dancing lights
tell me I am not alone.
I see them as fairies flying with their own purpose.
I hear their soundless sound and sing a silent song.

July 19, 1998

For Life and Beauty

Vapors drawn toward heaven by the warmth of the sun,
cooled to a colloid across the sky like grazing white sheep
or as dark columns that flash and roar their angry energy.
Cooled further into rain that makes earth fruitful
with wheat, corn, rice; with cattle, sheep, foul;
with deer, bear, wolf — and us.

Creator of landscapes, of music —
a stream sliding through a meadow, a forest;
a rolling river carving a cavern through painted rocks;
 a pond, home to lily pads, rushes, waving willows;
a lake lapping at rocks, at wooden boat docks;
arching ocean breakers buffeting a beach
the song of a waterfall, of a babbling brook.

The flowing fluid that makes us live,
the sculptor of scenes only it can give.
This singer of songs gives peace to our being.
It rules the world, all knowing, all seeing.

June 23, 1998

Flute Journey

Hear the songs of hidden spirits
    above a waterfall
Spirits of winds
    through woodland, along prairie
    across mountain, over ocean
of earth, water, fire
Spirits of Noble Indigenese from our beneficent land
    their tepees following bison
        that colored massive plains
    their cliff mounted pueblos spawning
        an ancient civilization
    their mounds for sacred grounds near
        fields they planted
    their longhouses and wigwams for hunters
        on land and water
Spirits of oak, maple, spruce suckling Mother Earth
of eagle soaring through the blue
of salmon sprinting up rivers to spawn
of wolf, deer, bear

These spirits rise from her wooden flute
    and fill our minds with dreams
These spirits dance their words through her
    and stories float on sonorous streams

September 18, 2003
Rev. 9/30/03, 10/8/03, 10/10/03, 10/30/03

Four Winds

I wake to the vigor of the morning wind,
listen to its song of flight and freedom,
smell the body breath it wafts
     of dew on thirsty loam,
hear its playful song among ash, maple, oak.

I labor to the cadence of the mid-day wind's
     working song
carrying pollen from corn stamen to corn silk
     from squash flower to squash flower
     from tea rose to tea rose,
drying freshly washed clothes,
propelling a sailboat across a rippling bay
     on port and starboard tacks.

I embrace the evening wind,
absorb its floral fragrance.
Caressed by its lovesong,
     I hold the warmth of another's hand.
We watch the white clouds grow rose and purple,
feel the cool wind invite us to
     share body's warmth.

My mind floats to the rolling rhythm
     of the night wind's lullaby,
drifts among dreams of yesterday's sunshine,
     of tomorrow's rainbows,
a lullaby written with star light
     on a staff drawn in moonbeams
     with the rhythm of planets and galaxies.

October 28, 2001
Rev. 4/18/02, 5/2/02, 5/7/02, 6/3/02, 10/23/02

A Grain of Time Suspended

Earth
Sleepy sun snuggles into bed.
Misty breath of her drowsy yawn
closes the rose, lifts robin's wings to nest,
draws the deer to evening drink,
lulls the wind to rest,
wakes the frog to chorus,
the firefly to fairy games,
the horned owl to hunt.

Heavens
The glow from sun's drowsy eye
colors cumulus clouds pink and purple
against a blue white sky.
Her eye quickly closes;
her last limb is tucked from sight.
Twinkling dots draw imaginary pictures.
Night's lantern bathes Earth in silvery white light.

Lovers
Sitting, side pressed to side
arms around waists
heads tilted to touching,
man and woman enfold the song of solitude,
embrace the intimacy of darkness.
Moonglow eyes sparkle replies to fireflies.

August 5, 2000
Rev. 11/7/00, 11/?/00, 8/18/02; 4/24/06

January

I resolve to be a better me
not to arbitrarily disagree
nor gorge on every food I see

I've got to lose my portly gain
reduce my heavy cardiac strain
take less in stomach — more in brain

I have to lower cholesterol
also reduce my alcohol
walk outside or in the mall

I have to learn to keep my cool
so I won't sound a blasted fool
dripping words from caustic pool

I'll give my wife much more respect
not deny her intellect
and, sometimes, tell her she's correct

My family has to have first place
above business, ball game or a race
spend more time being face-to-face

Resolutions add each New Year's Day
don't seem to do the things I say
it's a portrait of me like Dorian Gray

February 7, 2004

104

March

Welcome sweet springtime
      You greet us with snow.
We're waiting for flowers
      We want you to know.

Greet us with sunshine,
      We'll greet you with song.
The way you are going,
      You're doing things wrong.

We want warming earth
      Turning fields green.
But deep melting snow
      Just muddies the scene.

We've waited all winter
      To hear the lark sing.
It's been a long winter,
      Come NOW sweet spring!

March 28, 2005 Rev. 4/5/05, 11/09/05

Meeting

Two streams met
flow as one to the sea
Wind and cloud flow along
torrential tension
cloud is gone

December 4, 1998

Morning Song

A song sung in morning
flows 'til evening refrain
A song sung in sunshine
changes color in rain

A seed sown in sunshine
bursts open in rain
A seed sown in morning
warms 'til evening refrain

A caress in morning
grows 'til evening refrain
A caress in sunshine
shelters from rain

A life loved in sunshine
weathers well with rain
A life loved in morning
glows 'til evening refrain

2006

Motion

Rotating, revolving earth
turns me in celestial time
like round sounding words
spinning a rhyme.

Sun, part of a long, swooping arm
orbits me around Milky Way's core
like a glittering spark showered
by a rocket-driven pinwheel.

I circle in the cycle
of diurnal schedules
nights dark and light
days light and dark.

April 17, 2007 Rev. 4/18/07, 4/22/07

Morning Melody

Tall pines on the hill greet the sun
Streams lend rippling song
Earth, air and sea
Eagle, bear, deer
blink eyes open
Wind drones through a hollow log
whistles through trees
Morning moves to a silent drum
in soul-set rhythm

March 21, 2005 Rev. 4/13/2005

Summer Scorcher

1
Sputtering
Caldera
Ossifying
Reduction
Cauldron
Hope for
Evening
Relief

2
succulently
season in
sunscreen
saute
simmer
sear
sizzle

solar
sauna
sweat
shift to
shade

swim
soak
sip
snappy
soda

July 20, 2006 Rev. 7/24/06

The Awakening

Golden iris of morning's eye
peeks above the eastern hill
gold-lavender its cloudy brow
dew-damp its grassy hair
rustle-making song
      its morning yawn
Announce
the waking wonder

Sept. 1, 2003 Rev. 11/24/03

A Lanterne

the
gold bulb
in heaven's
socket lights the
soul

September 4, 2003

The Land's Blessing

Sky eyes straight plowed earth
Watches green life from its birth

Sun and moon measure time
Blossoms morph to pear, peach, lime

Sunflower follows sun's daily arc
Dew gives comfort when world grows dark

Earth Spirit blesses hands hugged by soil
Seed, sun, rain gift rewards of toil

Aura of peace crowns the land
Enfolds the soul of the working hand

The Sea

The rhythmic patter of the steadfast sea
speaks, if we listen, to you and to me
of island coves where pirates hid,
of porpoise, whale, seal and squid,
of kelp, coral, anemone and fern,
 of sailors in their last sojourn.

Waves that roll on toward the shore
know how the wind is keeping score
of games it plays upon the earth
as it travels around its girth;
the way it toys with sailing ships
by quickly changing how it grips
the gaff and topsail, gib and main
forcing trim, unfurl, trim again.

Far depths beneath the roaming sea
home to strange constituency —
worms, crabs, lantern and sightless fish,
some we would call quite ogreish.
Amazing things in the depths we find
in the ocean and in the mind.

February 13, 2005 Rev. 2/23/2005

The Third of Four Acts

The bright yellowish-green first curtain opened.
the eager sun warmed green shoots
scattered over earth-brown fields;
yellow daffodil, violet crocus
brightness greets the radiant sun;
red-breasted robin, crimson cardinal, blue-headed mallard
return from winter retreats, nest;
chicks, ducklings peck through translucent shells;
fox pups, fawn, foal, squirrel
enrich themselves from maternal bounty.

The mature green second curtain opened.
blossom wombs swelled with growing fruit;
fledglings learned to forage, hunt for food;
learned the way of the woods, the sweetness of the meadow;
cavort, race.

The orange-red-yellow-green third curtain opens.
nature's plenitude wanes;
robin, cardinal, mallard follow their compasses south;
hawk prepares feathers for cold;
fox prepares winter den,
hunts fattened game;
squirrel gathers nuts, lines comfortable hollow;
fur coats thicken.
The bleak brown curtain will close
until the fourth act
when the cast lives by its wits in the climax.

October 12, 1997 Rev. Oct. 31, 1997

The Titans

Fire in its belly
Earth rages
kicks Sea solidly
Sea roils — rises
Smashes a mighty fist into Earth's face
Tears away covering green
Swallows land
Buries debris in mud
       human and flora

Drags debris into his domain
Leaves salted earth dead
Poisons fresh water

The Titans become quiet
Sun weeps on the scene
Feet again move about
Hands dig with hope
Love searches for loved ones
       mourns the lost
Disaster becomes
a source of humanity

The Titans the source
     of life
     of death

February 27, 2005
Rev. 3/11/05, 4/13/05, 5/4/05, 12/27/11

Wake, You Sun!

Lift your golden eye
above its lid.
Dispel foreboding fog
 from harbor's mouth.
Lift the pervasive veil
hiding rocks and eddies.

Wake the wind
from pre-dawn sleep
to blow balmy breath
into sails of silent fishing boats.
Wake whiting, mackerel, bass
to fill empty hooks and nets.

Wake, you Sun!
Fishermen await you —
the young to start day's work,
the old to talk and warm
the salt in their veins.

October 29, 2006 Rev. 11/19/06

Waterfall

Would that I were a waterfall
nestled in the far ravine wall.
Like flowing crystals in the noonday sun,
I'd bounce from rock to rock,
sprinkle diamond dust on a cobweb.
Turned by a boulder, I'd spin smooth rocks
in a pothole ground round,
comb through emerald moss
on a long, flat shimmering face.
Roar my white-noise harmony
an aria in my opera.
Dive over a precipice
into a clear-eyed pool.
Offer a bath to dust-crusted hikers;
raise a rainbow in the late day sun
welcome deer, chipmunk, fox, wolf.
I'd sing my joy when welcoming rain,
gather the outflow from surrounding terrain,
pirouette 'round the rocks 'fore taking my dive,
and bless the water that keeps me alive.

April 16, 1998

Winter's Delivery

sooty city of yesterday
coated deep in swan's down
buildings, fire hydrants
wear hats of white fluff
windows wear white mustaches
cars now smooth sculptures

rattling rush
of the bladed behemoth
tosses alabaster clouds
rolling rumble
of spreaders
serve salt and sand
clatter, scrape of shovels
unbury walks, autos

autos hush along the road
headlights play on glistening glaze
tail lights glow like cherry stains
huddled shapes plod buried walks
slowly assail slippery surfaces

white dons
gray, brown, black
after the beauty of
pristine promises
live with delivered reality

January 29, 2004 Rev. 3/15/04, 4/24/04

POT POURI

A July Fourth in the Sixties

Flags and fireworks, fireworks and flags
High School football field
Lie on a blanket next to wife, children
        holding hands
First rocket announces the pyrotechnic show — BOOM!!
Second rocket bursts into a red-white-blue spray
Arcs of color mushroom down
Looking up we are immersed, enveloped
part of the glowing glory
Sparkling twirlers fly out from an explosive burst
into a sizzling white ball of curly-cues
Ends in a rain of sparkles and red embers
The aerial show continues
to light the sky above us
and we feel inside of it

We sit up for the ground display
White flashes race in opposite directions
along upper and lower lines
igniting an American Flag
        a red-white-blue
        "GOD BLESS AMERICA"
Roman candles, blazing pinwheels, multi-colored flares
An aerial and ground finale
        crackers, flaming streams
        glowing water fall, star bursts
SILENCE
Applause, cheers
Leave with patriotic pride

July 1, 2009

A New Year

An unblemished child
enters a living world
with bright eyes, rosy cheeks.
A bent-over, white-haired figure leaves.
Bent under the weight
of seconds, minutes, hours of 365 days.
Measures of the uncontrollable, unconquerable
dimension of our lives.
A resource not to be wasted.
It gives of itself —
takes for itself.
Not reusable, recyclable.
We march to its rhythm
burdened by baggage
buoyed by hope.

Many lanes to next year —
one speed, no passing.
Care at intersections
for those crossing, leaving, joining.
Pass calendar markers—
the temporal map for life's milestones.

East Meadow Library

The PR Office energy
    prepares programs for all.
Jude arranges lectures, exercise,
    writing workshop. — Hear the call!
Her schedule fills both time and space,
    sets a hectic office pace.
Linda handles any quirk
    ensures all the plans will work.
Doris's grace with graphic art
    gives fliers, bulletins appeal.
Laurence knows to do his part
    to make the programs real.

August 4, 2005 Rev. 9/8/2005

Hats

The hats I have has critics talking.
My lack-luster look makes them frown.
They want finer fashion when I'm walking,
riding, reading or being around town.

My Scottish tam taunts their senses.
My out-shaped outback brings looks of shame.
My floppy kibbutz forges fatal offenses.
I'm mindless of image; that's what's to blame.

My critics have bought me new chapeaus.
A broad-brimmed bushman for strong sun days,
an oilskin Aussie when rain or snow blows.
Now I must wear them 'til each sweatband frays.

Favorite Meal

Favorite —
the food or the gathering?
the flavor — family — friends?
Where in the scale —
a dish to die for
the gaiety of the group?
Mother's meal
served with a side-dish of love?

Dining with a special person
special birthday, anniversary?
Joy of Thanksgiving, Christmas, Passover?

Favorite meal —
a happy tummy taste
or a happening?

March 13, 2011

In the Cyclotron

Physicists use gradient and curl
      from vector calculus
to analyze field effects like
      electric and magnetic potential
to understand the pull of polarization
the ability of magnetism to change
the direction of a charged particle

Psycological fields in the media
pull on people's intellectual inclinations
with plagues of information, both right and wrong
intent on turning their mental momentum
toward a Mercedes, Mercury, Mazda
      a smart TV by Samsung, Sony, GE
      a smart phone by Samsung, Apple,
      Huawei
or a chosen political candidate

Marketeers and politicians
propel us around their cyclotrons
with infomercials, disinfomercials
to see what quanta of currency
what particles of power
they can create

October 30, 2004
Rev. 11/10/04, 10/24/21 m

Fisherman's Sea

Her salted breath gives urgent call,
      imbues one's lungs with vigor,
caresses every weathered face,
      belittles each man's figure.

She is home to swimming things,
      to porpoise, shark and seal,
to lobster, herring, hake and krill,
      each one another's meal.

A sorceress who changes state
      from peace to rabid fury
as soothed or taunted by the wind;
      who acts as judge and jury.

To this sea go fishermen,
      in sun and fog and rain.
Their mistress calls with scented breath
      and fills their lungs again.

With love and care they sail their boats,
      Harbor Hawk, Megamay.
They leave behind the harbor lights
      for wind and waves each day.

Tend trap or net at rosy dawn.
      Her bounty is their blessing.
Her challenge is their life reborn,
      her wiles are always pressing.

Then homeward bound to fireside
      with stories they will tell.
With leathered hands they proudly weigh
      the daily catch they sell.

Their nostrils hold her salted breath.
        Their lungs still hold her vigor.
When they talk of days at sea,
        they stand strong and bigger.

September 25, 1998; Rev. 10/6/98, 3/14/99, 2/25/01

Pinwheels of Light

Pinwheels of light
spun by a breeze of thought
focus the eye
in forehead's center
Seize the mind with
hands ripe with laughter
Weary words fall away
like autumn leaves
noisy in the ear
Nourish fresh leaves
that fly like whispered words
on an evening wind
Paste them into a mosaic
of a piece of time
ticking in a billowed cloud
that holds sunlight softly
Whimsically open a window
for a slim scribing beam
A beam whose warm words
excite imagination

May 20, 2004

Hate

Taught to pitbulls and children
makes them mean, makes them dangerous
And there's a curriculum

HATE 101
A course in importance
that is self-importance
that makes one better
 than those who
look different
pray different
talk different
walk different

HATE 102
A course in judgement
self-righteous judgement
against those who
look different
pray different
talk different
walk different

HATE 201
A course in power
power over people
people power that runs engines
engines of war

war against people who
look different
pray different
talk different
walk different

A curriculum with teeth
that rip the flesh off society
and chew on its bones

November 18, 1997

Silent Souls

Hear the silence of each anguished departed soul.
Hear the silence of a world watching with dry averted eyes.
Hear the silence of lifeless children's laughter unroll.
Hear the emptiness of mother's hearts after saying their goodbyes.

Hush, my child, die quietly
for a world that doesn't listen.
Pray, my child, 'til eternity
to a G-d that didn't listen.
Hear, Oh G-d, each tortured soul
searching for ears that listen.
We, oh Jews, have paid a toll
for a world that wouldn't listen.

Now listen
to generations of unborn children play
to wind through forests of family trees burned away
to countless tales of valor they lived each day.

Now say Kaddish for them when you pray

April 1991 Rev. Aug. 14, 1996 April 8, 2000

Kristalnacht — The Beginning

CRASH - CRASH - CRASH - CRASH
Rocks and bricks
Windows: Jewish-owned shops - synagogues
Scattering shards of glass
CLATTER - CLATTER
"Take what the swine stole from us!!"
Jewelry, furniture, suits, dresses, money
Synagogues, shops emptied, destroyed
Torahs, holy books piled in street

STOMP - STOMP - STOMP - STOMP
Hobnailed boots
Fiery eyes in stone set faces
HALT!
BANG - BANG - BANG -BANG
Doors quiver
Heraus Juden! Juden, heraus!
Shattered lives
Among shattered glass
Flaming torches
Flickering glow moves through streets
Torch piled Torahs, holy books
Synagogues — filled with Jews
Spirits
Fly up in acrid
Light obliterating smoke
Spirits carrying cries for help
Cries drowned by
SILENCE!

October 5, 2005 Rev. 10/18/05

The Ceiling

Stir thick new whiteness
Celebrate the ceiling
with new brightness
Also new brightness to
hat, hands, glasses
face, arms, shirt
pants, shoes
Also brightness to ME.

November 18, 1999

To Our Troops

You are the sound of a spear waiting for the throw
a taut bow loaded for launch
a sword and shield between home and harm.
You are brothers and sisters linked together
like a suit of armor ready to absorb an onslaught
the knight to force the battle forward.

Those at home with aging uniforms stored,
worn on days of veterans' memories,
have passed you a solemn heritage
you hold firmly and carry with honor
until you, too, shall pass it to ready hands.
A source of pride in your courage and manner.
You are stars in our Star Spangled Banner,

December 30, 2002 Rev. 1/25/03

Remembering a Valiant Life

Wake to
sunshine of a smile
smile of sunshine
voice of living song
song of a loving voice
warmth of human touch
touch of human warmth

Read books
Explore — challenge ideas.
Share brightness among the stars
with people on symbiotic orbits.

Wait to be lifted
from bed to wheelchair.
Wheelchair stroll,
greet neighbors.
"I'm fine. Thanks for asking.
"But are you over your cold?
"And your mother,
"is she still in the hospital?"

"Thanks for taking me to get my nails done.
"Now I'll check my e-mail.
I expect several replies."

Inside looking out
disregard skin stretched
over sinking frame.
See throb of living,
hear living song.

Heartbeat is rhythm,
art-of-living provides music,
 love and the joy of loving
write the words.

February 26, 2007
Rev. 2/28/07, 3/2/07, 3/5/07, 3/6/07, 3/13/07

What Color

What is the color of sadness
What is the color of joy
mother's love, father's pride
the laughter of a girl and boy
What is the color of a baby's cry
hands held in friendship, luck gone awry
What is the color of a nightingale's song,
a soprano singing a biblical psalm
What is the color of a Shakespeare sonnet,
the buzz of a bee with nectar on it
What is the color of a prayer for peace,
for hunger to end, for hate to cease?

November 7, 1999 Rev. 11/15/99, 6/26/07

To Minimalist

Minimilism
stretches
brain

My style
not same
Different brain
different game

Smooth rhythm soft sound —
Hard
Few words
found

Word-list
life's
events

Big
thought
little
package

Bare-bones
poetry
has
its
life

May 15, 2006

Worlds Apart

World beyond our world
time — energy — spirit
infinite non-dimensional intangible space
floats through atoms
surrounds galaxies

Belief — the transformer
mythology into fact
concept into truth
righteousness into *glory*

How many worlds beyond our world?
none?
one for each prophet?
one transcending
      all prophets?
      all metaphor?
      all comprehension?

    July 25, 2007 Rev. 7/28/07

Haze

Hides an unknown world.
Groping eyes and ears only grasp the unhidden.
      Merchants at their pushcarts and shops
            "Fresh fish! Today's catch!"
            "Bread, rolls — hot from the oven!"
            "Pots 'n pans! Pots 'n pans!"
      A horse clip-clops with a squeaky wagon.
      Bang, bang, bang — nails driven into the frame
            of a house that supplants a charcoal skeleton.
Some say they've seen shadowy forms
      outside the hiding haze curtain
      that stop, watch, beckon.
      Unanswered, they fade behind the curtain.

I open the cover of a gray morning
      to read the introductory lines
      of another enclosured day.
There is the ritual glance at the imprisoning white curtain.
      I stop! A shadow beckons to me. I start toward it.
      My mind says, "Don't go. You don't know what's there.
      No one else goes there. Don't be different!"
The shadow beckons again.
      My heart says, "There is more to the world
            than these houses, pushcarts, and shops,
            than these grappling merchants and toilers."
I follow. I reach the white curtain to the unknown.
      It isn't there! The curtain had opened on an inviting garden.

I see a fantasy of violets, buttercups, daisies,
      bridal wreath, weigela, wisteria.
      The fragrance of eucalyptus calms and invigorates.
The shadow behind the curtain waits, watches.
The curtain parts and I follow my guide along a rising trail
      over rocks and tree roots, through thick forest.

A stream splashes around smooth stones,
      beneath willow, cottonwood and fern.
      It's water sparkles without sunlight.
      I touch it's cool caress, taste its primal purity.
What is this mountain that gives it birth?
The trail rises steeply into the hiding haze.

As I continue, again the white curtain opens onto new perspectives.
      I see a spring issue from between rocks
      pouring life's experiences
      into a bottomless pool of time,
      nourishing absorbent minds
      making them adornments for the world
      as rushes, lilies and lush grass beautify a mirror pond.
Now I challenge the hidden hazards,
      enthusiastically follow the beckoning guide, climb.
I climb past birch and fern,
      leave the valley behind.
      No more starlings flying in flocks.
      Toadstools grow, moss on trees and rocks.

Mud and loose earth make my feet slip.
Low-hanging branches and exposed roots
      reach out support, offer a grip.
I reach a small meadow rounded by oak and fir trees,
      played with by daisies, buttercups, cornflowers.
I sit beneath a wizened oak, sung to by working bees.
Rest and food restore my body's powers.
Refreshment served by a nearby spring
      cools my body, clears my head
      to bring to my heart the hymn
      of the mountain's breeze.
I cross the meadow and climb once more.
Trees become shorter and soon cease to grow.

I reach a ridge. The mountain offers another
          sparkling spring from which
          my soul quenches an inherent thirst.
I look down and see far beyond
          the tawdry town as in a poem:

          I see fields of grain, grazing cattle and sheep,
          towns at crossroads with steeples up high,
          rows of markers of eternal sleep,
          cities whose buildings caress the sky.

I look up and see the mountain's gilded peak.
The shadow-guide, gone, left a smile in the sunlight —
          the sunlight that melted the haze
          from my mind.

                              January 2, 1998

UN Meeting

          Assembly perched
          on branches
          decorated by early Spring.

          Can one comprehensibly translate
          the ebony crow's raucous caw-caw
          for the sweet throated thrush?
          Do the multilingual
          mockingbird and catbird
          understand the innuendo?

          The red-winged blackbird reiterates its
          territorial claim
          and warns

against intrusion.
The macho crow protests:
      There are no borders in the air.
But he knows if he gets too close,
beware, beware.

Resolution by the sparkling white dove:
      We shall respect each other's territory.
Green and red parrot
black macaw with long yellow bill
white cockatoo
repeat in unison.

Sharp-eyed falcon, hawk,
eagle silently watch
from perches on high.
They know
that yea's
from all the lower feathered flock
make harmony
but cannot withstand
their veto.

March 21,1997
Rev.: August 22, 1997

Snow Satan's Blessing

Sooty city of yesterday
coated deep in swan's down
Buildings, fire hydrants
wear fluffy white hats
windows wear white mustaches
mud-spattered cars
become smooth sculptures
A primal scene for
poets, painters, musicians
for ski slopes, ski shops

The rattling rush
of the bladed behemoth
tosses alabaster clouds
conceals cars
Autos hush along the road
pack the unskimmed layer
headlights play on glistening glaze
tail lights glow like cherry stains
Rumbling salt trucks, sand trucks
spread their stuff

Shovels clatter, scrape
expose walks, autos
overtax hearts
We clamber across uncleared walks
slowly assail slippery surfaces
broken bone falls on ice
Time changes white to
gray, brown, black
Listen to the beauty of
pristine promises
Live with delivered reality

January 29, 2004

WRITING

A Poem

A garment formed to fit my soul —
    adjusts its breadth, depth, girth
    as each turn of thought I discern.
Its designed drape gives
    new warmth to words
    new perception to phrases
    new depth to dreams.
It was drawn in discovery
    patterned from passion
    sewn with serendipity.
It dresses me for new skies
    dances me into new dimensions.
A garment whose metaphoric embroidery
    gives resonant color to pastel reality.

December 20, 1998
Rev. December 31, 1998

Reading Poetry

Each poem its own rhythm
Each rhythm its own emotion
Each emotion its own place in my life
Each poem I enjoy reflects
    something from my life
in the way Frost, Pinsky or Whitman
    perceives life
I file these new reflections in a growing me
A "me" growing in questions
Each question its own rhythm

May 13, 1998 Rev. 5/15/98

Poetic Epicure

Savor sounds of Frost
Complex simplicity
sensualizes the mouth
teasing taste buds
with assonance, consonance, meter

Ponder willful words of Poe,
Masticate detailed description
'til sweet juices
tantalize the appetite
with unexpected flavors

Whirl rolling rhymes of Whitman
 kneaded and baked
into layered scenes
flavored with alliteration
sweetened with soothing vowels

May 10, 2002 Rev. 10/10/02

Two-Line Poem

Brilliant black-eyed susans swaying after a summer shower
Children's amazed eyes watching aerial artistry

March 28, 2006

Conception

I draw my mind down to a vacuum,
let light illuminate the void,
make it a play place for thoughts.
Thoughts that ruminate or softly scamper
play shadow figures on my consciousness.
They settle comfortably
        like an egg entering the womb
or flounce around like agitated spermatozoa.
A virile sperm mates a promising ovum.
Their DNA join, split, develop a skeleton,
add organs, nerves, brain,
muscle, skin, emotions, sensuality.

It absorbs my energy.
I feel its weight, its movement, its growth.
I write as a robot controlled
by signals from its umbilical cord.
My words are its birth canal.
I hold it, caress it, put it to sleep.
It awakes, cries for attention.
I feed it, clean its waste, change it,
help it develop, shape its character.
I show it off to my friends.
They praise the pulchritude of my progeny,
the performance of my parenting
and render remedial recommendations.

October 21, 2002 Rev. 1/3/03, 5/22/03

The Taproot Workshop (For Older Writers)

You ask how come I bounce out of bed on Tuesday mornings?
How come I don't lie there deciding if I really want to get up?
How come there is a spring in my step instead of the usual shuffle?

Well, Tuesday is my Taproot Workshop,
my meeting with my mental mentors,
my spiritual supporters,
my soul's energizers.

On Tuesdays, we share our newly birthed words
We pour life's loves, losses, laughters into a cauldron.
We simmer, stir, sample, suggest, ingest, digest.

You ask about learning at our age?

We may have slowed,
but each mile makes the next mile easier.
There is no age to energy,
but age has to switch it on.
Thought doesn't get arthritis,
unless you stop thinking.
The pulse of idea comes from the rhythm of the soul,
not from a pacemaker.

Together, we are an amplifying plasma.
We transform a ray of thought into a laser beam —
brilliant, coherent, focused.
Together, we are explorers of our uncharted selves.

March 31, 2001 Rev. 7/?/01

The Way of Words

Words walk with slippered steps
silently sort into strings of sound
      their mood in their music
           their reason in their rhythm

Words have wheels
      roll down a raucous road
along a stream teaming with stories
They toss a line
      hook a slice of life
shape it
      write its sound
           birth it

Words whirl in the firmament
arrive like light gathered from distant galaxies
give glow to their flow into weaver's web
enticing lead
      intriguing middle
           kicker conclusion

December 5, 2007

The Writer's Club

Words flow from hidden grottos
Life and dreams intertwine
Thoughts, when penned, make a rhythm

Wanting their reflection in clear glass
No judgement
      just the sight of their sound
      energizing ears
      to color friendly faces
Wanting to weave and roll on playful waves
with words from unfamiliar caverns
They lead my reigns where writers read
They the riders
      I the steed

June 7, 2008 Rev. 9/20/11

THANKS AND FAREWELL

Adieu

Now you've read the work I've done,
Some of it serious, some of it fun.
I hope you're glad you spent the time
Reading my poems in freestyle and rhyme.
They give a picture of my soulful side
To solve the problems I had every day
When sun and rain respectively tried
To brighten my life or shade in grey.

www.ingramcontent.com/pod-product-compliance
Lightning Source LLC
Chambersburg PA
CBHW031415120626
46545CB00006B/2145